HOW TO TRADE SHARES

GROW YOUR RETIREMENT FUND & TRADE YOUR WAY TO FINANCIAL FREEDOM

Aberdeen Trading

ABOUT IAN ABERDEEN

After Ian Aberdeen graduated from Melbourne University he managed his family business and then operated a business consultancy for the next for 45 years, one of the highlights of which, during the reign of President Marcos, involved overseeing some of the large scale Philippine economic infrastructure projects for the World Bank. He has traded shares and operated a family superannuation fund for the last 30 years, and is a long-standing member of the Australian Technical Analysts Association. Over the last 10 years he has developed some simple share-trading tools which generate daily reports on trading results and identifies shares to sell. Prior to the Global Financial Crisis (GFC) hitting home he nervously sold his entire portfolio based on *The A-Line Trading Strategy*. That decision proved to be one of the best moves of his trading career.

HOW TO TRADE SHARES

An introduction to trading Australian shares

Ian Aberdeen

Published by The Countryside Academy Pty Ltd 2014

www.aberdeenstockmarkettrading.com

Copyright © 2014 The Countryside Academy Pty Ltd

This publication is copyright. All rights reserved. Except as permitted under the Copyright Act 1968 no part of this publication may be reproduced, stored or transmitted by any means, electronic or otherwise, without the specific written permission of the copyright owner.

Aberdeen Trading is a registered trading name of The Countryside Academy Pty Ltd

First Printing: 2014

ISBN 978-1-291-98161-2

The Countryside Academy
PO Box 4099, 631 Glen Huntley Road
Hopetoun Gardens, VIC 3162

Ordering Information:
Special discounts are available on quantity purchases by corporations, associations, educators, and others. For details, contact the publisher at the above listed address.

CONTENTS

About Ian Aberdeen ii
Foreword vii
Preface ix
Why share trading? 11
    our mantra: 12
What are the first steps? 13
    The 1st Myth 17
How Is money made? 19
What is a share? 21
What is a dividend? 22
How are new shares issued? 23
    The 2nd myth 25
Where do I begin? 27
Share trading goals 29
Isn't share trading risky? 31
What is paper trading? 34
    The 3rd Myth 35
What do I need to start Trading? 37
Which shares should I buy & how many? 41
When should I sell shares and how? 44
Can I keep it simple? 48
How do I get The A-Line Strategy? 49
Appendices 51
Calculating Compound Interest 53

Notes 55
Notes 56

FOREWORD

I can count on one hand the amount of people who stand out as having given me knowledge that has taken me leaps forward in how I conduct business. Ian Aberdeen is one of those people. He's also my wife's uncle and the possessor of a very funny and dry wit. And sheep. He loves his farm and his sheep.

When I was first told about him I was informed he was breeding a self-shearing sheep on his farm that would save the wool industry and farmers huge amounts of time and money. I was also told on the same farm he was experimenting with a new drought-resilient grass that provided good nutrition for his sheep. Having a rural upbringing myself I told myself 'this is a man I must meet'.

Our first meeting was at a family Christmas gathering in Melbourne. Ian looked every inch the farmer; tall with a solid build and pragmatic. Our first conversation soon turned to the markets and investing. Little did I know that I was talking to a heavyweight on the subject. I must have held my own because since then I have been privy to priceless one-on-one trading lessons as well as the inner workings of a mind that ceases to rest with age.

The business we co-founded, called Aberdeen Trading, was pitched to me by Ian one morning in his Kilmore office as we sat discussing the stock market. In that moment the voice in my head told me to grab on with both hands as opportunities to work alongside people like Ian don't come along every day. Since then my trading and general business acumen have vastly improved and continue to do so. I hope you find use in Ian's words and wisdom as I have done on my journey as a trader.

Iain McLean

PREFACE

I received encouragement to write this book, and decided that I could generalise to the point where my particular hardware, software, skills and trading methods were not made clear. But I have gone the other route and described how I trade shares – not giving all the theory behind why I trade this way but enough of how I trade to allow the reader to visualise themselves at the computer.

There are millions of share traders around the world, each trading in a different way, using software packages and electronic brokers in ways I do not. If you become a share trader you will find that the industry is always changing and you need to keep running to stand still. My words below will soon become half forgotten, but I hope you learn something from them. Just so long as you can get some facts, some trading rules, and a glimpse of the fear and envy that invade share traders emotions, I will have been privileged to capture your attention for an hour or two.

Enjoy.

Ian Aberdeen

WHY SHARE TRADING?

I started writing this book just after the Federal Budget had been launched in May 2014. The budget was full of deprivations which the Abbot government said we had to have. The Australian public had recently voted in this new government at a democratically run election, and the public got the budget they deserved. But they did not like it. Such is life, as Ned Kelly is reported to have remarked standing at the gallows. We'll all be 'rooned said Hanrahan before the year is out.

The purpose of this book is to show you what careful share trading involves, how a series of risk controls can protect your capital gains, and what levels of return you can expect to achieve.

A great way to get your mind into the investment challenge is to go back 2,000 years and read the parable of the talents. The internet will find you a rather academic description of that parable, which finishes with the confronting warning that "*to those that have shall be given, and from those that have not shall be taken away even that which they have.*"

The parable of the talents is a good money management lesson. Making money is one thing but using your money to make more money is better and those that have money will inevitably find a way to take it of those that don't. This millennia old parable has been the backbone of tax laws for as long as there have been tax laws.

As a child born onto a dairy farm with a bank mortgage at the start of the great depression I can relate to the parable quite easily, But Australians born in the next generation are clearly finding this century mean and scary coz things aren't what they used to be. Today it's no longer smart spend all you earned, coz tomorrow we die, stuff the kids, why should we leave anything for them. The Global Financial Crisis (GFC) that we had to have, put an end to that lifestyle, at a time when grey power was retiring and governments were finding that they lacked the income to keep the oldies in good health. As life expectancy stretched out towards 90 years, the superannuation funds that were supposed to sustain retirees were looking less and less likely to do so.

It's one thing to avoid leaving an inheritance, but another altogether to live in poverty for your last 10 or 30 years.

So. I trade shares. I have traded for over thirty years and made myself financially stable. I've also made my children financially stable but it doesn't stop there. You have to pick up the gauntlet and carry on my work where I leave off otherwise the money will run out.

OUR MANTRA:

If I can make a profit from share trading without losing those profits, then I will be able to live better for longer into my retirement, and won't have to rely on the government or relatives.

So what is the first step? Read on...

WHAT ARE THE FIRST STEPS?

To invest, you need something to invest with so if you haven't already got some money put away safe then you'll have to begin saving some.

STEP 1

The first thing to do is to develop a life-long habit of saving. A few coins a week at first and more as your income grows. Just don't spend everything that comes your way. Start a savings account.

Remember though, such persistent saving to build your retirement fund requires a good attitude. Along the way you will have banks and stores trying to tempt you with credit cards and store cards. If you do one thing above all else, avoid using credit cards. They use your debt to make the banks money and once they have you in their debt it's hard to get control of your money back.

Start an action plan. Write down how much money you make each week, how much you need to spend on food, travel, clothes and other things and see what's left. This is a budget. If you find you're not saving as much as you need to, think what you can spend less on (food, travel, clothes etc.) and make a new target.

Income: $_____

List your expenses:

Total Expenses: $_____

Savings: (*income – expenses*) $_____

STEP 2

The second thing to do, once your savings reach a threshold amount which we'll talk about later, is to invest your savings to get it growing at a reasonable rate. For the moment let's think about earning a 8% per annum return on your savings instead of the miserable 3 % which the bank pays in their savings account.

STEP 3

The third thing to do is to keep your savings growing for several decades. The whole point of this is to enjoy the benefits of growth with compound interest.

I'll explain compound interest soon – it's one of the big secrets you need to grasp.

In the meantime, keep a lookout for penniless old people. You don't want to end up like them do you? No – I thought not. Use their example to encourage you to start thinking about what you spend your money on and saving more.

~

So if in five or ten years' time you have built up a savings fund that is available for investment, the two major alternatives to leaving your funds in the bank, will be to invest in property or shares.

Let's talk property first.

I happen to own our family house and a small farm almost by default, and have not developed a policy to suggest to others. I know that our accountant encourages our children to buy their house first and pay off the mortgage, before investing in any rental property.

On the other hand a recent paperback by a self-made successful property investor recommends to borrow as much as you can from your bank to buy a second property for investment, because that way you will soon be earning enough from capital gain to pay them both off.

But quite recently I have read another book by Philip Anderson in which he documents plenty of evidence showing that real estate prices move in an 18 year cycle.

I therefore suspect that successful property gurus may have invested at the right time in the cycle, because we all know stories about a house, or other property not selling for years, and the bank not giving loans to buy real estate at present.

There are lots of points of view to confuse you. That's one lesson you will learn – how to read lots of books and articles and find the core that links them all.

Anyway this book is just about the other alternative to investing in shares. One thing I can vouch for is that you can sell shares a lot faster than real estate.

I became a kind-of-guru one day in November 2007 when I sat at my computer and entered sale orders to my internet share-broker to sell my whole share portfolio. It took about two hours to type in all the details of the shares held in three family portfolios, and by the 4pm market close all transactions were complete. We were out of the share market just before the 12 months share market crash of 2008 when many others lost half their capital.

Don't be fooled by my "Little Jack Horner" story (look it up on the internet). There are serious risks confronting any share investor, and this book describes a share trading system which sets up a whole series of risk control tactics to earn an income from shares.

Not everyone has the life circumstances or the temperament to trade, and recent surveys show that only a low percentage of Australians are successful share traders.

THE 1ST MYTH

Growing your wealth and becoming rich isn't about making more money.

It's about protecting the money you already have and using it wisely to make more money.

HOW IS MONEY MADE?

The first lesson in understanding what money is and how it's made is to come to terms with the fact that money has very little meaning.

This can get very confusing very quickly so think of money as a score card. Sport uses score cards like how many points your team got or how many runs they made or who played the least amount of strokes in golf. These scores have the same meaning as money – they tell you how good or bad something is performing. Money simply tells you how much value something has got.

IF you want to be really academic then this is the definition of money:

> *"Money is a transferable recorded token of value for goods and services."*

In business money isn't the main reason a company does what it does, a company is driven by the passion and enthusiasm of the people that work there. The amount of money the company makes is a score card telling everyone else if the company performed better than last year or not.

Money itself is worthless because it needs to be attached to something of value to have any worth, and in monetary terms value = price.

Once you understand that very important lesson you will see that what matters is doing your job well not chasing the money. The reason being that chasing money will inevitably bring out negative emotions that soon prevent you from doing your job well – and then nobody will want to pay you anyway...

So, back to your question: how is money made?

Every country in the world has its own money called currency. When a product is bought in one country and sold in another it's value remains the same but the price may be different in the new currency. This difference is called the exchange rate.

Global currencies are what are called Fiat Money. Fiat in Latin means "*it shall be*". They are called fiat money because government decide how much the value of a currency is worth. They do this to control economic growth to allow stability for businesses so we can hopefully all live better lives.

To get more money into the economy banks use what is called Fractional Reserve Banking. This works in a relatively simple way:

When a high street bank deposits $1,000 in the central bank, the central bank allows the high street bank to then lend $10,000 to its customers even though it doesn't have that much to lend. This is because the fees charged to the customers (*you and me*) pay the high street bank's debt to the central bank.

Let's look at it another way:

A country's central bank (*the bank that makes the major decisions, not the bank you have your savings account with*) gets money into the economy by lending it to high street banks (*the ones you have your savings account with*).

This puts the high street banks in debt to the central bank.

High street banks pay back the debt the central bank by passing on the debt to their customers by things like fees on credit cards.

Banks put themselves in debt to make money. They are businesses so they need to recoup their debt and make profit. They do this by charging their customers (*you and me*) fees. Banks need you to go into debt so they can charge you more fees to grow their business.

Remember Step 1 on page 15? Do you understand why credit cards are so bad now?

WHAT IS A SHARE?

A share, or stock, is the cornerstone of our free enterprise system. Every business has shares. If you own shares you own part of a business.

Shares come into being by their parent companies need to raise capital to grow their businesses. If new business needs money to fund get a product off the ground and into stores they can issue shares. If they issue 1000 shares to 1000 people willing to put up $10 per share, or venture capital, by selling the shares the company will raise $10,000. The investors who now own the shares are stakeholders in the business and each own 1/1000 of the company.

Consulting 1000 people for every decision about the business would be impossible so a board of directors is elected. The board members are picked by shareholders and receive votes per the amount of shares they own. If one board member has one share, he will have one vote whereas if another member has five shares he will have five votes. The board then elects a chairman to oversee the process of decision making. They also appoint officers who may not sit on the board but who are required to report to the board either monthly or quarterly on the progress of the business.

Once a year the board will present the annual report to the shareholders where shareholders can have their say about decisions made or motions proposed for the company. Part of this annual report is the disclosure of the profit and loss of the business.

People invest in businesses to make money. As a shareholder in a business you can grow your wealth in one of two ways, either by the value of the stock you hold increasing, or by the payment of a dividend.

WHAT IS A DIVIDEND?

If the company in question has profits of $1,500 after paying taxes and all outstanding bills, or in other words 15% on its $10,000 capitalisation, that shows positive growth for the business.

$$\$1,500 / \$10,000 = 0.15 = 15\%$$

The board of directors can then vote to reinvest the money in the business or to pay it out to the investors. As all investors like dividends, and board members know this, a common route is for boards of directors to payout $750 in dividends and plough the remaining $750 back into the business to keep the growth positive.

The dividend payout for this example is simple, the total dividend amount $750 divided by the 1000 shares outstanding.

$$\$750 / 1000 = \$0.75$$

This gives a dividend payment of $0.75 per share. If a shareholder has five shares his dividend payment will be $3.75, whereas a shareholder with only one share gets $0.75. This represents a 13% return on investment.

$$\$10 / \$0.75 = 0.13 = 13\%$$

Another intangible return is that the $750 put back into the business would hopefully increase the company's value, in turn increasing the value of individual shares so that the original share price of $10 becomes $11. This is called price appreciation.

HOW ARE NEW SHARES ISSUED?

Our imaginary company has now been in business for a few years and experiencing solid growth year-on-year. Shareholders enjoy good dividends each year and the value of the stock is rising well. As happens with most businesses, to stay ahead of the game, a new product is launched. This needs a larger factory to house the expanding workforce and new machines but $20,000 is hard to find.

Banks hold one option but the money borrowed is charged interest and the banks typically don't like long-term investments like this and if they were interested might demand a place on the board with voting rights. After all that hard work, you can see why the board of directors might be reluctant to ask a bank for the money.

There is another way. The board declares it will issue a further 3000 shares, 2000 of which will be sold immediately with the remainder held in in reserve should the business want to raise more money in the future. These new shares hold the same privileges as the original shares. A motion is put to the shareholders and is passed.

Existing shareholders are given the option to buy new shares as a discounted rate prior to their sale on the open market. Each share held by a shareholder entitles that shareholder to exercise his right to buy one of the new shares at $10.50 before they go on sale on the stock exchange at $11.

If this right is exercised, a shareholder with one share now worth $11 can buy a second for $10.50. He would then own two shares at the equivalent of $10.55. The right is said to have a value of $0.25. If he sells the two shares on the stock exchange for $11, their present market value, he stands to realise price appreciation in terms of cash from the sale.

Some shareholders may be unwilling or unable to buy more shares so they can sell their rights. The formula for working out the value of rights is as follows: The exiting market price less the subscription price.

$$\$11 - \$10.50 = \$0.50$$

Divide the difference by the number of old shares required to buy a new share plus an additional one.

$$\$0.50 / (1+1) = \$0.25$$

The value of the right is $0.25.

The rights have time limits and when those limits expire the company finds that all have been exercised except for 100. In the process the company raised $ 19,950 to expand its factory and has 3900 outstanding shares.

$$3000 - 2000 - 100 = 1900 \text{ shares sold.}$$

$$1900 \times \$10.50 = \$19,950 \text{ new capital.}$$

THE 2ND MYTH

If you can follow simple mathematics and understand why:

$$\$11 - \$10.50 = \$0.50$$

And:

$$\$0.50 / (1+1) = \$0.25$$

Makes:

$$3000 - 2000 - 100 = 1900 \text{ shares sold.}$$
$$1900 \times \$10.50 = \$19,950 \text{ new capital.}$$

Then you can follow most, if not all, of the mathematics required to start share trading.

WHERE DO I BEGIN?

Several decades ago while working for The World Bank in the Philippines I learned a method of describing a project. It allows the project manager to see the activities and outcomes that he will manage, and the financial and social goals that the project is expected to achieve. It is also a valuable document for those wanting to monitor your progress such as your bank manager or your partner.

We used to set the Logical Framework out on a large sheet, with three columns. We pinned the completed Logical Framework to the office wall and kept it updated for everybody to see.

The first column contained the hierarchy of Goals, Activities and Outcomes that you will find below.

The second column showed achievement indicators and milestone dates for each item in column one.

The third named who was to monitor progress towards those achievements and how often.

Whenever I was given the job of monitoring from the third column, I always found my presence was unpopular: an unwanted pest. But someone other than the manager ought to be watching and reporting.

I strongly recommend that once you get the hang of the logic below, you should decide the correct goals and activities for your own circumstances and set them out on a sheet of paper in the three column format. It will soon become a powerful tool for problem solving, and there will be problems ahead.

The most disappointing solution which you may decide or may be forced onto you by others is to stop share trading. That outcome is contrary to the usual recommendation to never give up, just sort out your problems and keep trading.

It is well worth committing your finished Logical Framework to memory. That way when you identify that your share profits are heading the wrong way.

My trading system is designed to alert you daily when such problems arise.

When you feel the surge of fear, because you have memorised the Logical Framework, you are still able to visualise your action plan that will lead to a diagnosis of cause and best corrective action.

SHARE TRADING GOALS

Below is an very simple example of a Logical Framework:

Goals, Activities & Outcomes	Requirements, Indicators & Milestones	Responsible Person & checks
Learning money management	Reduce my debt on my credit card	Me. Check account balance weekly.
	Get rid of my credit card	Me. Cancel card when balance is $0
Start budgeting	use spreadsheet from www.aberdeentrading.com	Me. Save receipts and log expenses.

    Below I have set out a basic definition of what we consider to be a good set of goals, activities and their requirements for share trading.

    You can either use these to build your own Logical Framework or pick the ones would feel apply to your objectives and mix them with your own goals.

Financial Goals

- To earn a yearly average return on my capital involved of 8% or better.
- To never lose capital when trading.
- To conduct the share trading using appropriate financial entities.

Social Goals

- To use a trading system that suits my time availability and lifestyle.

- To develop a new financial skill that I can use after retirement.
- To steadily build a retirement fund that will prove adequate income for our life expectancy.
- To fully document the share-trading strategy and tactics, so that the family can learn and use it in the future.

Activities and Outcomes

- Study books and newsletters which teach conservative methods of trading Australian shares, and then come up with a written trading plan.
- Acquire the necessary hardware and software for electronic share trading, and then do some dry runs with paper trades to prove my system.
- Commence real-time share trading in a small way, following all the buy, sell, and risk control tactics built into my trading system.
- Check my capital gains and dividends daily, and if my results are satisfactory steadily build my share investments to the current level recommended for my shares to cash ratio.
- Keep accurate buy and sell records for presenting to my accountant at the end of each year.

Requirements

- Sufficient time available for me to manage this share-trading system properly.
- Good hardware and software installed to allow me to work efficiently and accurately.
- A room where I can work privately and quietly.
- Business entities properly established, as recommended by my accountant and solicitor.

ISN'T SHARE TRADING RISKY?

I have a close relation who is a world-leading medical researcher. He states bluntly that share trading is gambling, not to be practiced.

I once heard a preacher say that "It is not that Christianity has been tried and found wanting, it is simply that it has been tried and found too difficult."

That is how successful share traders view their business. They know there are real risks and that some people lose capital to the extent that they will never trade shares again. The solution is to develop a trading system that contains a series of risk controls – what came to be known in World War II as the Russian defence i.e. defence in depth.

At Aberdeen Trading we have a very tight set of money management rules and operate with a high degree of risk management. Taking from the history books we have called our system of deeper and deeper control levels the Russian Defence. What follows is a list of the seven risk controls we use, each one creating a further barrier to risk.

The first control is to have a written plan, after the style of the Log Frame above with each goal and activity expanded into a short text. This will allow rapid trouble-shooting, and the Australian Taxation Office requires owners of Self-Managed Superannuation Funds to create and follow a written management plan.

The second control is to only use the maximum allowed capital to trade shares when your system is generating the profit levels you seek i.e. cash percentage control.

Our proprietary indicator the A-Line is used to read the mood of the market, and decide what cash percentage is appropriate. We publish a weekly newsletter which begins with a Dow Theory analysis of the Australian share market, and a reading of our proprietary A-Line index of trader sentiment, before than suggesting an appropriate percentage of cash to hold in reserve given those readings.

The third control is to buy mostly Class A shares (*definition below*) that show a rising price chart.

We adhere to the well-known motto that the trend is your friend, so never trade against the trend. A macro market uptrend is called a bull market, but within the chart of that market index (*I use the All Ordinaries Index*) there will be mini and larger downswings known as corrections. The trend is your friend motto strongly warns against trading those downtrends, and I do not.

The fourth control is to use software like the Trader's Workbook available from Aberdeen Trading which draws a daily chart of accumulating trading profit from capital gain and dividends so early warning of trouble is clearly seen. They say a picture is worth a thousand words and the sight of a plunging profit I find to be very motivating. We expect it to sometimes happen, and we will survive if we respond quickly.

The fifth control is to score the daily and weekly charts of all shares held at least each weekend, and to sell shares with a deteriorating chart. I have developed a scoring system which we teach to A-Line Newsletter subscribers available on the Aberdeen Trading website. It is reliable enough to allow rapid sorting.

The sixth control is to choose the most probable and avoid the least probable trade. A major part of that process is to check both weekly and daily charts, with a few of the many technical indicators turned on.

The seventh control is to avoid risk by not putting all your eggs in one basket just in case the cane basket falls apart. The share trader's version of this risk control is called position sizing, and I will get to that shortly. Don't worry, it's not as intimidating as it sounds.

A thoughtful reader will have detected that there is always an elephant in the share trading room; namely the threat of a sudden trend reversal which you did not see coming. Older traders resign themselves to the truism that you cannot predict the future direction of the share market or of individual shares. Short-term traders who sit in front of a computer all day keep looking for signals to sell before a price crash does them much harm. We are building a list of those tools. That list includes the Multiple Moving Averages

That brings me to a very special method of guarding against sudden price loss – The Stop-Loss. You will be able to explore the nature and use of this tool with your internet broker, both when you own shares in a company and when you are trading Contracts For Difference (CFD's).

Swing traders used to sell shares short, but a new method of selling CFDs is now used to trade bear markets when the macro trend of the market is down. CFD trading allows you to make more profit because you are using borrowed money, but it equally allows you to lose more money because your losses quickly multiply. CFD's are a high-risk proposition and not something the novice trader should be considering. Only when you have significant experience should you begin thinking about CFD's and at that point there are a lot of dedicated books on the subject by people who are experts in using CFD's.

Finally we come back to the trend motto again. If you buy as share with a falling share price you are clearly playing chicken with the market. You are daring the market to keep pushing the price lower and destroying you capital. That is a risk I am not prepared to take, so I only buy shares with a rising price and sell those with a falling price.

WHAT IS PAPER TRADING?

There is a lot to be said for getting ready to trade, and then learning the system by trading shares on paper before committing your hard earned to the market.

Paper trading involved pretending to buy and sell shares 'on paper' and you only need a few basic things to get started:

You give yourself an imaginary trading fund of say $50,000 to buy shares and make money.

You use a trading journal to write down all your share purchases and sales in and record your profits and losses.

All you do then is follow a trading strategy like The A-Line Trading Strategy and begin paper trading.

Some people paper trade for a month before actually trading in real-life whereas other people paper trade for months or a year. The whole point of paper trading is that you learn how to make profit form trading shares and make your early mistakes without having your money at stake.

Once you are consistently making profit and have ironed out your mistakes you're ready to trade in thr real world.

Even Paper Trading shares gets a bit tricky if you really want to simulate the real world and I have a short module which you can acquire via the instructions at the back of this book.

THE 3ᴿᴰ MYTH

No successful person ever got rich quickly.

That's why the saying "easy come, easy go" is true.

It's much better to get rich slowly

Getting rich slowly lets you learn about how to best make money and how best to protect it.

WHAT DO I NEED TO START TRADING?

This book is describing share trading done from a computer, placing buy and sell orders through an electronic broker. Such brokers do not provide advice on which shares to buy or sell, but charge quite low brokerage fees for the service.

When you learn to become a competent trader, your trading costs will be less than trading through a traditional broker, or from placing your funds in a managed fund.

There are some basic tools that you cannot do without and I have listed them next:

Trading Funds

It is possible to calculate what level of funds you need to trade in the market and make a nominated profit before you can justify the capital costs of setting up and the operating costs of dealing yourself through an electronic broker.

You can begin very slowly at the bottom and learn your way using smaller amounts with a small trading account of $5000 but you will need to do a lot of homework on reducing your operating costs by finding reliable charting software and data feeds that are as cheap as possible.

This method allows you to get your trading psychology well defined by the time your trade account has a substantial dollar amount in it.

Putting $20,000 into your first trade can be an anxious moment for some people. Be warned though, the costs incurred with trading make maximising profit on this type of small fund very prohibitive.

A more ideal fund size to begin trading is somewhere between $15,000 and $50,000. Some trading coaches insist you should not start before your trading assets are around $200,000 to $300,000 but this would keep most people out of the market altogether.

A Computer & Software

You will need a computer and they come in many guises these days. Even though you probably have a good computer already to make things easier and reduce mistakes have found that using three screens is the easiest way to work.

As a retiree I trade shares from my home office and use a desktop computer built by our local computer shop. It has three screens driven by a video card in the box, and I can open programs on all three screens or even pull programs from one screen to another.

Two screens will also do but only using one screen makes things hard as you need to look at data on one screen while entering data into another. You can usually run a second screen from a laptop without any major issues but to have three screens you will need a bigger video card.

Your lifestyle and your office space will determine your computer selection, but it must be loaded with Microsoft Word and Excel, or equivalents. Whatever your configuration you will need a fast, reliable internet connection.

The second capital purchase will be a share charting program that can download the closing prices from a data source after the share market closes each day.

I use a program called STEX Charting, in association with their matching STEX Portfolio Manager. The latter allows me to answer any difficult questions our accountant asks when preparing our tax returns.

There are many charting and portfolio management programs around, and each will quote a setup cost and a monthly data download fee. Because I use the Multiple Moving Averages (*MMA*) Oscillator in STEX as a key indicator I look at other software packages and find that their charting screen either does not present the MMA or their option does not give the clean li;nes I can get on STEX.

The last two systems you need will be the cheapest to set up and run i.e. MicroSoft Excel and an exercise book. My business, Aberdeen Trading, has developed a share-trade recording and charting program called The Trader's Workbook that runs on Excel. You can design your own version or buy a copy of ours with a manual. We rule vertical columns into our exercise book and call it our order pad.

Trade Account

The third system you need is to sign up with an electronic share broker. Most of the big banks have one. You will find that each has a particular way of handling your share trading funds.

My arrangement with NAB is that I run several accounts in our local bank, which are directly linked to special cash accounts run by the broker NABTrade.

Before I can buy shares I must transfer adequate funds from the bank account into the NABTrade cash account. Again your electronic trader will quote you their brokerage and other fees.

Education

You can probably guess what else you need before share trading can commence and become profitable – ongoing learning by reading and doing.

You could spend a lot on buying books, subscribing to newsletters and attending conferences. Share trading is a huge industry with all sorts of marketing campaigns hunting you down and bombarding you with offers.

I have certainly found that I can only take so much knowledge from each news source but I need useful content and I have come to bin newsletters that go on for many pages without giving you a message you can act on tomorrow.

We formed our own company called Aberdeen Trading to describe a relatively simple and low-risk method of trading through a series of books, manuals and a short but meaty weekly newsletter.

And Finally...

And finally the first and last requirement for getting ready to trade shares is to find and rely on the advice of a good accountant and a solicitor, especially if the two already know each other and work for some joint clients.

Share trading is a business, with government laws on tax returns and many other aspects. You need advice from your accountant and possibly a special financial adviser within that firm on whether share trading is an appropriate activity for you and your family. Then you need more advice on a partnership, or family trust or self-managed superannuation fund should be established as the business entity which conducts the share trading.

By hiring a good solicitor and accountant team you can reduce your tax burden by using the best set-up for your business. A good tax lawyer is worth his weight in gold when it comes to end of financial year tax-time.

WHICH SHARES SHOULD I BUY & HOW MANY?

Let's start with the "how many" question.

To keep it simple, we will assume that you have $100,000 available for share trading. I use several rules to finally decide the maximum number of shares of one particular company I should buy for the share portfolio.

Rule One

I take a close look at the All Ordinaries index (XAO) of the Australian share market, and at our proprietary index (The A-Line) of the mood of local market traders. Based on that analysis I decide the current risk level of holding shares in that market, and decide on what percentage of the $100,000 should be held in cash.

If I decide to move to holding 50% cash and the current cash level is 40%, then I must sell enough shares to raise that 10% extra cash. If the situation is vice versa, then I must spend some of the available cash to buy shares. Each Saturday the A-Line Newsletter from Aberdeen Trading suggests a cash percentage to hold each week.

Rule Two

I have decided to divide my share investment funds into four categories:

- 10% of the fund will always stay in cash
- Maximum 5% can be invested in promising spec stocks (Class C shares) which do not yet pay a dividend
- Maximum 10% can be invested in shares paying less than 3% dividend (Class B shares)

- Maximum 75% of the fund to be invested in Class A shares paying a dividend (preferably fully franked) greater than 3%.

Rule Three

I adopt the well-known practice of putting a limit on the percentage of the fund which can be invested in any one company.

This is called position sizing.

If for example I choose a limit of 3.75 % per share code, that would mean that when rules one and two allowed full investment, I could invest $3,750 into each of 20 Class A shares.

Rule Four

When Rule 1 requires more than 10% of the fund to be held in cash and I find a promising new Class A share to buy I can spend say 1% of the fund to bring some shares into the portfolio now, and build the holding to the maximum 3.75% if that becomes possible and desirable later on.

This is called pyramiding.

I also follow the reverse procedure of selling part of a shareholding if its quality is fading and cash has to be generated,

Now let's look at the "which shares" question.

You will have gathered from the four rules above that the type of shares you want to buy are Class A shares with a sound background and a regular dividend averaging more than 3% per annum.

My approach is to keep collecting the code of such shares into a Prospect List. Then if the time comes when the four rules say it's time to buy more shares, I will bring up the chart of each share on the list with the MMA turned on and I will score both the daily and weekly charts from -5 to +5 based on whether it is in a rising, sideways or falling trend.

The four rules will tell you how much money will be available to buy each share, and so you can calculate how many shares to process through your exercise book.

For each share you will divide the total dollars per share by the current price per share to get the number of shares you will buy.

It may all seem a bit of a worry, but we discuss the buying routine quite regularly in our newsletter and you will master the routine fairly quickly, if not all the nuances.

The simple fact is that most trading mistakes are made when traders sell shares rather with the buying.

WHEN SHOULD I SELL SHARES AND HOW?

There are several reasons why you need to sell shares, but let's begin with my favourite saying:

"Sell and regret it, but sell"

Not only does it apply to the great share crashes that start the big bear markets, but nearly all of the circumstances described below require you to take prompt action if you are to follow the logic which you set out in your Logical Framework.

Reason 1

The reason why my written share trading system requires all shares to be sold to cash at the start of a bear market is that big bear markets cause the price of all shares to fall, and you have no idea how far they will go.

The Aberdeen Trading weekly newsletter on that occasion will urge all subscribers to move to 100 % cash.

There used to be a saying that nobody rings a bell at the top of the market, but that isn't necessarily so any more. I know of two algorithms which have done and continue to do just that, and our firm developed and owns one of them which we call The A-Line.

Of course this first rule only applies to the whole market as an Australian–wide bear market gets underway. For most of our trading career we are dealing with macro and micro rises and falls in the price of individual shares.

Reason 2

We need rules on how to read the price trend of individual shares, and technical analysis books contain thousands of pages on this subject.

Charles Dow (*of Dow Jones fame*) taught us that a price chart which shows three trend types. Rising peaks and troughs show us a rising trend, whereas falling peaks and troughs are a falling trend.

The third trend goes sideways with level tops and bottoms, and is regarded as a price trend top or bottom or a consolidation pause in an uptrend or downtrend.

I often use two of the simplest technical indicators: the straight line and moving averages, both of which are covered in the textbooks and training courses.

The saying that *'the trend is your friend'* assumes that you already know how to determine which of the three possible trends a share price chart is exhibiting. I also developed a method for scoring price charts from +5 to -5, as a shorthand way to pick the best to worst shares that I hold and also have in my prospect lists.

Another very definitive way of spotting when a share price has started a downtrend, is to look at the daily and weekly charts with the MMA turned on. As soon as band of six trader moving averages switch from their top position in an uptrend, to reposition under the six blue average lines of the investors, the share should be sold. We can teach you further finesse on that rule if you become a paid up member of our Aberdeen Trading newsletter.

Reason 3

The rule for beginners is to sell shares which meet one of two criteria:

- Shares where the price is in downtrend, because they are generating a loss for you;

- Shares which are in a slight upwards or sideways trend and by comparison with another share in your portfolio or prospect list are inferior, so that if you made a swap you would avoid the opportunity cost of holding onto your share with poorer performance.

Those are the reasons which I recommend a beginner to follow, but I should flag for your future use the news that there is another dimension to buying and selling shares. That dimension is called CFD's which I spoke about in brief earlier. All I want to say here is that CFD's allow you to make more profits for less outlay, but unless you keep your wits about you they also allow you to lose money much faster.

Which brings us to the process of selling shares. With the old-style full-service broker you picked up the phone and asked him to sell, and he did the rest. Using my electronic method I have to work through a process while avoiding any mistakes, in the belief that I am saving on brokers fees.

The place where I review the performance of shares held is a particular sheet in my Traders Workbook. A copy of that software is free to our newsletter subscribers. I am also able to look up information on shares bought, sold and held in two other places :in the records held by my electronic broker (in my case NABTrade) and in the Portfolio Manager software which matches my share charting package (in my case STEX). With the three screens run by my desktop I am able to view both my Trader's Workbook and individual share charts to make accurate decisions.

The sequential tasks involved in selling shares go something like this:
- Assemble an accurate list of shares currently held in each portfolio.
- Identify which of those shares are performing poorly.

- Check your cash percentage position to see whether you should hold the present level of your kitty in shares, or sell some or buy some more.
- If you need to sell some shares, identify which shares you should sell to increase your cash percentage to the mew target.
- If you should buy more shares to reduce your cash percentage, identify both the poorer shares you will sell anyway, and the better shares that you will buy.
- Then pull out your exercise book you use as your Order Pad and list the shares you will sell, along with the number of shares to be sold, and the price per share if you will sell to a limit price rather than "at market".
- On your computer open the window of your electronic broker, at the Place Order position, and start entering your share Sell orders. On each occasion you will nominate the limit price below which the broker cannot make a sale, or alternatively you will enter a sell at current market price order.
- As each sale is executed by your broker, a sale invoice will be sent to you, which you should print off.
- Finally enter the details of each sale into your Trader's Workbook, and into your computer based Portfolio Manager if you have one.

CAN I KEEP IT SIMPLE?

The answer to this question is a categorical Yes and No with every reservation. Remember your Shakespeare:

> In peace there's nothing so becomes a man
> as modest stillness and humility.
> But when the blast of war blows in our ear,
> stiffen the sinews, summon up the blood,
> disguise fair nature with hard favoured rage.

A share trader has to have a brave heart. Follow the rules with discipline and they will do what they were designed to do; that is to protect you from excessive risk and allow you to grow your savings through share trading. They are simple rules to follow.

By share trading you are taking on a task of complexity and difficulty, and you're doing it because in this day and age of the 21st Century your superannuation and old age pension are unlikely to support you and your family in the living standards you have currently.

I have been lucky to have lived in a time when the government could afford to pay an old age pension that allowed a good standard of living for those people who didn't have enough savings. For you though it will be very different. If you don't start saving now for your future your old age will be very bleak indeed.

This is my legacy to you.

You can succeed in building a family retirement fund through share trading but only if you follow the rules set out above, and you keep learning through reading and experience.

HOW DO I GET THE A-LINE STRATEGY?

Sign up for a subscription to The A-Line Newsletter though our website at:

www.aberdeentrading.com

You will receive:

- The weekly A-Line Newsletter.
- Our Subscriber's Manual along with our Trader's Workbook software and manual for managing your trades.

You may decide to test the trading system and our tools by making paper trades, or to immediately set up to begin buying and selling shares.

APPENDICES

There is always more to learn. Here we provide you with more in-depth data to help your decision making process.

These appendices are here to provide you with more detailed information to aid in your decision making process and allow you to carry out your own due diligence prior to joining the A-Line Newsletter subscriber community.

CALCULATING COMPOUND INTEREST

The goal of the share-trading system described above is to achieve a higher rate of return on your assets than you can earn from bank interest. But the glittering prize comes from just retaining your annual profits in the fund, as you do during the accumulation phase of a superannuation fund, and letting compound interest work its magic.

The following table compares the growth of an investment fund at three rates of compound interest, if you start year one with $200,000.

	Int. rate 3.5%	ROI of 8.5%	ROI of 13.5%
Starting value	$200,000	$200,000	200,000
Terminal value after 20 years	$397,958	$977,954	$2,522,000

Formula for the Terminal Value of a Unit Annuity = $[(1 + i)^{n-1}]/i$

If you did reach a retirement age of 65 years after 20 years growing your fund like this, you could have some confidence that you could live until say 90 years of age on a retirement fund of $2,500,000 especially if you planned to continue your share-trading system.

By comparison, you would probably feel obliged to find part-time work, if your retirement fund had only grown to $400,000.

NOTES

NOTES

www.ingramcontent.com/pod-product-compliance
Lightning Source LLC
Chambersburg PA
CBHW072251170526
45158CB00003BA/1048